Step into Science

What's the Problem?

How to Start Your Scientific Investigation

Kylie Burns

Science education consultant: Suzy Gazlay

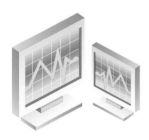

Crabtree Publishing Company

www.crabtreebooks.com

Crabtree Publishing Company

www.crabtreebooks.com

Author: Kylie Burns
Series editor: Vashti Gwynn
Editorial director: Paul Humphrey
Editor: Adrianna Morganelli
Proofreader: Reagan Miller
Production coordinator: Katherine Berti
Prepress technician: Katherine Berti
Project manager: Kathy Middleton
Illustration: Stefan Chabluk and Stuart Harrison
Photography: Chris Fairclough
Design: sprout.uk.com
Photo research: Vashti Gwynn

Produced for Crabtree Publishing Company by Discovery Books.

Thanks to models Ottilie and Sorcha Austin-Baker, Dan Brice-Bateman, Matthew Morris, and Amrit and Tara Shoker.

Photographs:
Corbis: Louie Psihoyos: p. 15
Discovery Photo Library: Chris Fairclough:
    p. 28 (center right)
Getty Images: Ariel Skelley: p. 8; Stockbyte: p. 10;
    Hulton Archive/Stringer: p. 24 (center right)
Istockphoto: Benedek: p. 4 (bottom left); Sean Martin:
    p. 6 (left); Duncan 1890: p. 9
Samara Parent: back cover, p. 1 (top)
Shutterstock: front cover, p. 1 (center left and right), 3,
    6 (bottom center), 11 (bottom), 23, 24 (bottom left),
    25 (top right), 27 (center left), 28 (bottom left),
    29 (right); Cathy Keifer: p. 7 (bottom right); Mandy
    Godbehear: p. 12; Julien Bastide: p.13 (bottom);
    Kiselev Andrey Valerevich: p. 14; Joe Gough: p. 20;
    Lisa F. Young: p. 21 (bottom); Jay Bo: p. 25 (center);
    Rob Marmion: p. 26 (bottom); Morgan Lane
    Photography: p. 27 (center right)

Library and Archives Canada Cataloguing in Publication

Burns, Kylie
        What's the problem? How to start your scientific investigation? /
Kylie Burns.

(Step into science)
Includes index.
ISBN 978-0-7787-5158-8 (bound).--ISBN 978-0-7787-5173-1 (pbk.)

            1. Science--Methodology--Juvenile literature. 2. Science--
Experiments--Juvenile literature. I. Title. II. Series: Step into science
(St. Catharines, Ont.)

Q175.2.B87 2010   j507.8   C2009-906463-4

Library of Congress Cataloging-in-Publication Data

Burns, Kylie.
    What's the problem? How to start your scientific investigation / Kylie Burns.
        p. cm. -- (Step into science)
    Includes index.
    ISBN 978-0-7787-5158-8 (reinforced lib. bd.g : alk. paper)
    -- ISBN 978-0-7787-5173-1 (pbk. : alk. paper)
    1. Science--Methodology--Juvenile literature. 2. Science--Experiments--
Juvenile literature. I. Title. II. Series.

    Q175.2.B87 2010
    507.8--dc22
                                            2009044175

Crabtree Publishing Company

Printed in the U.S.A./122009/CG20091120

www.crabtreebooks.com   1-800-387-7650

Published in Canada
Crabtree Publishing
616 Welland Ave.
St. Catharines, Ontario
L2M 5V6

Published in the United States
Crabtree Publishing
PMB 59051
350 Fifth Avenue, 59th Floor
New York, New York 10118

Published in the United Kingdom
Crabtree Publishing
Maritime House
Basin Road North, Hove
BN41 1WR

Published in Australia
Crabtree Publishing
386 Mt. Alexander Rd.
Ascot Vale (Melbourne)
VIC 3032

CONTENTS

THE SCIENTIFIC METHOD

Have you ever been in an elevator? The **scientific method** is like an elevator—you enter at the first floor and take the elevator up. The elevator passes one floor at a time, and you get closer and closer to your final stop. Sometimes, however, the journey takes you back down before you continue on to reach your destination.

In the same way, following each step in the scientific method is important for making scientific discoveries. Sometimes, though, scientists have to stop, go back, and think again before they continue.

▲ This scientist is studying a fossil. She is looking for answers to questions about the past.

In this book you will learn how to identify a problem, how to ask **measurable** questions, and how to gather information to guide an experiment.

The Truth
One of the first scientists to describe the scientific method was Alhazen (965-1039). He said it helps us know "the truth" about the world.

Beginning Your Scientific Investigation

Be curious! Questions can come from anywhere, anytime. Questions help scientists make **observations** and do **research**. Science is all about problem-solving!

Making Your Hypothesis

So, what's next? You have a question, and you have done some research. You think you know what will happen when you perform your experiment. The term **hypothesis** means educated guess. So, make a guess and get started!

Designing Your Experiment

How are you going to test your hypothesis? Designing a safe, accurate experiment will give **results** that answer your question.

Collecting and Recording Your Data

During an experiment, scientists make careful observations and record exactly what happens.

Displaying and Understanding Results

Now your **data** can be organized into **graphs, charts**, and diagrams. These help you read the information, think about it, and figure out what it means.

Making Conclusions and Answering the Question

So, what did you learn during your experiment? Did your data prove your hypothesis? Scientists share their results so other scientists can try out the experiment, or use the results to try another experiment.

THE WONDER OF IT ALL

Do you ever wonder what happens inside a tornado, or how a firefly makes its light?

Scientists are curious about the world. They are also problem-solvers. That's why scientists ask questions—by discovering a problem, they can find ways to solve it!

Scientists question things they can observe—that is, what they see, hear, feel, taste, touch, and smell.

Here are some questions scientists often ask:

what? **when?** **where?** **why?** **which?** **how?** **what if?**

Sometimes, scientists try to find out what something IS, but finding out what something is NOT can also lead to discoveries!

▲ Some people find tornadoes so interesting they get very close to them. These people are called storm chasers.

"Men love to wonder, and that is the seed of science."

Ralph Waldo Emerson

Inspire to inquire!

Do you ever ask questions that no one seems able to answer? What do you do? If you're a scientist, you get curious! Reading books and magazines, checking Web sites, and talking with experts are great ways to do scientific research.

Word Up!

The word science means "knowledge." The scientific method is not just about *what* is discovered, but *how* something is discovered, and what we do with that information.

▶ What makes this firefly light up at night? Be a scientist and do some research to find out!

AM I CLEAR?

Questions must be measurable. That means they must be detailed, carefully worded, and can be tested with an experiment.

Imagine that your great aunt Hilda offers to knit you a new sweater. Would she ask about your favorite color if she wanted to know how long the sleeves should be? No! She would ask "How long should the sleeves be in order to fit you from shoulder to wrist?"

◄ Scientists are serious about making things measurable and specific. Even knitting a sweater for someone requires careful measurements to be sure it will fit.

Then, like any good knitting scientist, she would measure twice, and knit once!

Without measurement, you can't do science. Without a **specific** question, there is nothing to measure!

Isaac Newton

Isaac Newton was a scientist who once observed an apple falling to the ground. He was curious to know why things fell with such force. He wondered if the same force was keeping the Moon close to Earth. In order to prove it, he designed a measurable test that led him to one of the greatest discoveries of all time—the force of **gravity**!

SCIENTIFICALLY SPEAKING

Curious minds question everything—but not every question is scientific!

It is important to start off with a scientific question. Scientists have an idea about what they think will happen. Then they try to prove it by doing an experiment.

Questions help us plan a useful experiment to test an idea. What scientific questions do you have? Remember, if you can't test your idea, other scientists can't test it to prove you right!

There are some questions that are not measurable. The question, "What happens to plants when people talk to them?" sounds scientific, but how would you test it?

◀ Will plants grow better if they're talked to? Do an experiment to find out.

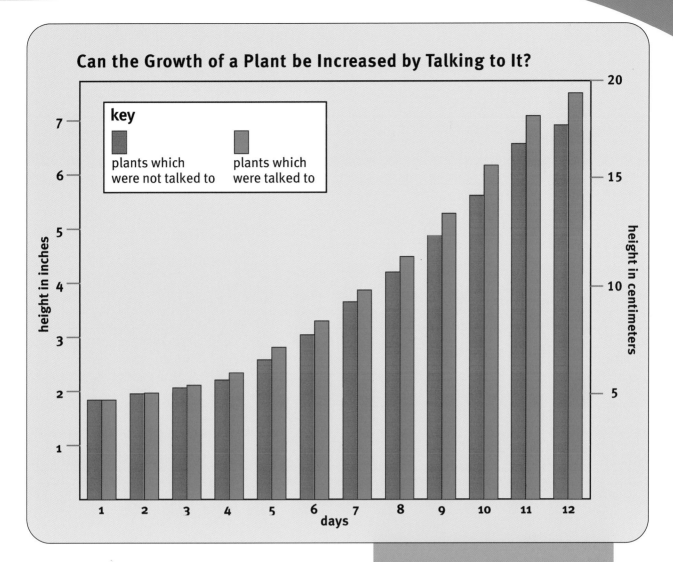

Can the Growth of a Plant be Increased by Talking to It?

key

■ plants which were not talked to

■ plants which were talked to

height in inches

height in centimeters

days

▲ This graph compares the growth of plants in an experiment. Which plant grew tallest?

It can't be answered scientifically because it wouldn't be possible to measure what is happening to the plants. They don't talk! They can't share their feelings!

Instead, try asking "Can the growth of a plant be increased by talking to it?" Then the plant's growth can be measured and compared to the growth of plants that were not talked to.

CARE FOR A SAMPLE?

Scientists often talk to other scientists about their ideas. Sometimes, they try out their question on a group of people. These people can be friends or strangers, old or young, and male or female. They also don't have to be scientists! A group like this is called a **sample**.

Sampling is useful because sometimes it is hard to tell whether your questions are specific, measurable—or even safe! Other people can tell you whether there are any parts of your question or idea that are confusing or difficult. If your question leaves them asking more questions, then it's not scientific!

▼ A scientist may use a sample group like this one to find out if a question is specific and measurable. These children are saying YES!

Cousteau's crusade stopped the experiment!

Safe Science

Scientists look for ways to solve problems. But sometimes, the problem is the question! In 1960, a group of scientists were planning to find out what would happen if dangerous chemical waste was dumped into the Mediterranean Sea near Corsica (see below). **Oceanographer** Jacques Cousteau had a problem with their question. He wondered how the researchers would control how far the chemical waste might spread, and how it might affect the sea. To Cousteau it seemed like an idea that could harm people and the environment. So, he and many other concerned people demanded that the experiment be stopped–and it was! The other scientists had thought they had a good question, so they hadn't tried out the question on a sample. If they had, they might have realized that their question was not measurable because it was not specific. By questioning a sample of people, big problems can be avoided.

You should always discuss your question and plans with a parent or teacher. They will be able to tell you if there are any parts of your experiment that will be difficult or dangerous. You can then make changes to ensure your experiment is safe and effective.

SILLY OR SCIENTIFIC?

Sometimes, people who are curious don't take the time to be scientific. Larry Walters wondered if attaching **helium** weather balloons to his lawn chair would allow him to float. He did not research his question. He also didn't test his question on a sample. In fact, there was very little science involved in his investigation at all.

Armed with the balloons, snacks, and a pellet gun, Larry Walters planned to prove that he could float just above his street in California. But when he launched into the air on July 2, 1982, air currents took him up so high that an airplane whizzed by. The pilots spotted him out the window!

▲ Scientists are always careful and prepared. This scientist is wearing protective equipment during an experiment. Safety comes first!

► John Ninomiya soars above the ground during a cluster balloon flight.

By popping some of the balloons with his pellet gun, he managed to come back down after many hours, but the first people to greet him were police officers. Larry could have been seriously hurt, or caused others to be injured.

John Ninomiya

John Ninomiya spent many years researching the science of balloon flight. He became a licensed hot-air balloon pilot and had over 400 hours of flight experience before he tried to fly using helium balloons on April 15, 1997. Since then, he has completed over **40 cluster balloon flights** safely and scientifically! Who do you think was the better scientist? Larry Walters or John Ninomiya?

LET'S EXPERIMENT!

Cleaning Dirty Water

Problem

Much of the water you drink came from rivers and lakes. One of the ways water companies make the water clean enough to drink is **filtration**. What sort of filter do you think they might use?

Materials:

- ☑ soil
- ☑ water
- ☑ bucket
- ☑ three jars
- ☑ three empty plastic bottles
- ☑ paper coffee filter
- ☑ dishcloth
- ☑ small kitchen sieve or strainer
- ☑ scissors
- ☑ stick
- ☑ measuring cup

1 Mix equal amounts of soil and water in your bucket. Stir it well with a stick. Ask an adult to cut the tops off the plastic bottles, about four inches (ten cm) from the neck. You will use these as funnels.

2 Put your coffee filter into the plastic bottle funnel. Put the funnel into the mouth of a jar.

3 Put your dishcloth into another plastic bottle funnel. Put the funnel into another jar.

4 Put your kitchen sieve into the third funnel. Put this funnel into the third jar.

5 Pour one cup (250 ml) of muddy water into each of the three funnels. Pour slowly to prevent the funnels from overflowing.

6 Leave your jars with their filters for an hour before looking at them. Which filters have the most water or the most mud? Now look at the water in each jar. Which looks cleanest?

What Do You Know?

Perhaps you've used a net in a pond or tide pool and noticed that the water goes through it, but stones and weeds do not? Or maybe you've seen your parents making coffee with a coffee filter to keep the grains out of their beverage? Did this help you think about which filter would work the best?

Warning:
Water companies do other things to make dirty water clean. Do not drink the water left after this experiment.

SURVEY SAYS!

There are many ways that scientists collect data. A **survey** is a scientific research tool made up of questions. Surveys are used to gather information about people's feelings, behaviors, or experiences. Survey data can help scientists see patterns and focus their research.

Survey questions must be carefully designed, without **bias**. If your questions are biased, it means you are letting your own opinions show in your questions, or you are giving people hints about how you want them to answer. Bias causes your data to be incorrect and unscientific.

▼ Surveys must be designed to get a person's honest opinion. Survey questions should not try to encourage someone to answer in a certain way.

It's a Fair Question

Look at the following two survey questions—can you tell which one is biased?

Question 1

"Like most people your age, do you forget to do your homework all the time?"

• Yes / No

OR

Question 2

"How often do you forget to do your homework?"

• Never? • Once a week or less?
• Between two and three times a week
• Between four and five times a week

If you think the first question is biased, you're right!
The second question does not try to influence anyone to answer a certain way.

Biased Survey Questions:

Don't you agree that keeping birds as pets is a problem?

There are many people that think using sunscreen is silly. Are you one of them?
YES/NO

How do you rate this new soda pop flavor?
GOOD/EXCELLENT/THE BEST EVER

Unbiased Survey Questions:

What is your opinion about keeping birds as pets?

Do you apply sunscreen before going outside?
NEVER/SOMETIMES/ALWAYS

On a scale of one to ten, one being bad and ten being excellent, how do you rate this new soda pop flavor?

BEWARE!

Questions can help us make sense of information. Sometimes, people make false scientific claims. Don't just believe what you hear—investigate!

Science is always growing and changing. There have been many times in history when something that was believed to be true proved to be false. New **technology** has allowed people to conduct scientific experiments like never before.

Marshall and Warren

Doctors used to believe that stomach **ulcers**, or sores, were caused by stress and spicy foods. However, in 1995, Dr. Barry Marshall and Dr. Robin Warren discovered that **bacteria** cause ulcers, not a person's lifestyle. Their incredible discovery helped to change the way doctors treat ulcers. Marshall and Warren won a **Nobel Prize** for their work. They asked deeper questions and found new answers!

▲ Spicy food was once thought to cause stomach ulcers—but it doesn't!

Separate fact from fiction!

Just because something is reported in the newspaper, on the radio, on television, or on the Internet, doesn't mean it's true. Always look for proof of good scientific research!

▲ Don't be fooled—not everything you hear, see, or read is true!

LET'S EXPERIMENT!

Marble Ramp

Problem

Marbles tend to roll around, but not always in the same way. How do you think slope will affect the way a marble rolls?

Materials:

- ☑ a marble
- ☑ several books of the same thickness
- ☑ a paper towel tube
- ☑ masking tape
- ☑ a marker

1 Find an uncarpeted floor with plenty of space. Put a piece of masking tape on the floor and mark it with an "o." This is your starting point. Place your marble on the tape and let go. Does it roll? How far? If it does roll, take another piece of masking tape and stick it where your marble stops. Mark the tape with the number "1."

2 Now place one of your books on the floor. Lean your paper towel tube against it so that it makes a closed ramp. Make sure the top of your ramp is over your starting point.

3 Now place your marble at the top of the tube and let go. Watch to see where it stops this time and mark the spot with a piece of masking tape. Write the number "2" on it.

4 Put another book on top of the first book and make a ramp again. This time the ramp should be steeper. Let your marble roll down the tube again and mark the place where it stops with a piece of tape. Write the number "3" on it.

5 Add another book to the pile and try again. You can keep going until you run out of books. Make a ramp as steep as you can so the tube is almost upright. What does your marble do then?

What Do You Know?

If you've ever played a soccer game, you'll know that the field is flat. If you've ever tried playing soccer on the side of a hill, you could probably guess what would happen in this experiment!

STICK WITH IT!

When scientists have a question to answer, they work hard to find the best way to test their idea. Sometimes, they easily move from one step in the scientific method to the next. More often, they must repeat their work over and over before reaching a final result. Other times, their questions remain unanswered, even after years of research and study.

Jonas Salk was a scientist who believed he could find a way to prevent the spread of a disease called **polio**. He researched and tested many possible combinations for a **vaccine** that would protect people.

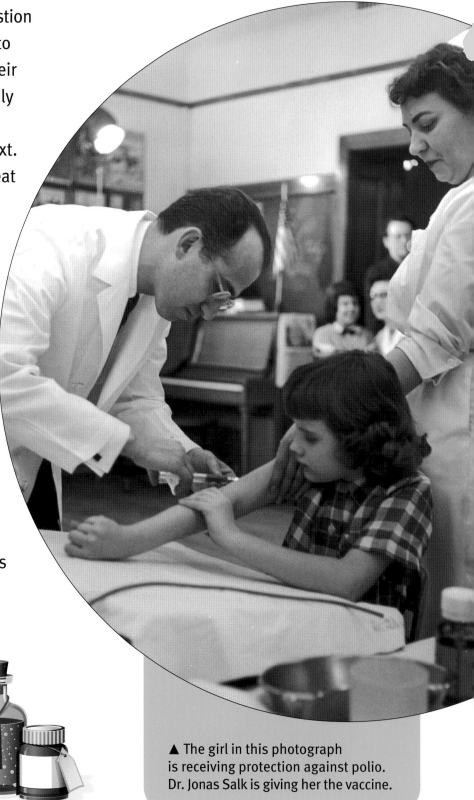

▲ The girl in this photograph is receiving protection against polio. Dr. Jonas Salk is giving her the vaccine.

He began his research in 1947. After seven years of careful scientific experiments, he finally discovered the vaccine. Because he didn't give up, children and adults today have protection against a terrible disease.

▼ Will we ever know how sea turtles find their way back to the same beach where they were hatched? Maybe someday you will find the answer!

Turtle Power

Some scientific questions remain unanswered for a long time. For example, research has shown that when female sea turtles are ready to lay their eggs, they return to the beach where they were hatched. No one knows for certain how sea turtles find their way back after swimming thousands of miles around the world.

ONE MORE QUESTION— NOW WHAT?

Good questions lead to good research and scientific experiments. The next step in the scientific method is to make a guess about what your experiment will prove. This is called the hypothesis.

▼ When we make a prediction about what will happen, we create a hypothesis that can be tested.

The hypothesis is often called an "educated guess." That means you take your experience, research, and understanding, and you make a **prediction** of how your experiment will turn out. A lot of times, your hypothesis will be right, but there are also times when you will be wrong. That's how science works!

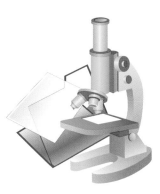

▼ There are many opportunities to think scientifically about the world around you. So get going and start wondering!

Turn it Around

You can turn your scientific question into a hypothesis by making your question into a **statement**. Let's go back to our plant question: "Can I increase the growth of a plant by talking to it?" Now change it to a hypothesis: "Talking to a plant will increase its growth." You are ready to test your hypothesis!

KEEPING A JOURNAL

Imagine that you discover treasure after searching for many years. How do you remember where it is buried so that you can return later to dig it up? You draw a treasure map! It must have all the important details about **how**, **where**, **why** and **when** you made your amazing discovery. For scientists, that treasure map is called a **journal**.

Science is meant to be shared!

▲ You can illustrate your journal with photographs and pictures.

A journal can be anything from a scrapbook, to a binder with lined paper, from a computer file, to a notepad! The important thing about a journal is that it is where scientists record everything about their experiment, from beginning to end.

In this step you can use your journal to write down any observations or questions you have about the world. Then you can write down what you find out about those questions during your research.

Here are some Hot Tips for Keeping Your Journal:

- Make sure you write the date every time you use your journal;
- Make sure you write clearly, so that you'll be able to read your notes later on;
- If it helps, you can draw pictures or diagrams, but avoid fancy handwriting or any decorations that might make your journal hard to read;
- Try carrying your journal with you—then you can write down any observations or questions you have straightaway.

◀ Write your journal notes clearly and carefully.

My Science Journal

Cleaning Dirty Water

✳ Day 1. March 14, 20/

Question

Today when I was drinking some water I wondered how it got clean enough to drink. I think water companies must filter it to get the dirt out. I wonder what would make a good filter?

Research

I used the Internet to look at what might filter dirty water. I used these websites: www.

Hypothesis

Procedure

TIMELINE

Below is a list of scientific discoveries and inventions that were the result of asking important questions!

Year	Discovery or invention	Who asked the question that led to the discovery or invention?
1450	The printing press	Johannes Gutenberg wonders if a machine could make life easier for people to communicate messages and information on a large scale.
1608	The telescope	Hans Lippershey wonders if a special lens could allow people to see the stars and planets up close—from Earth!
1714	The mercury thermometer	Daniel Gabriel Fahrenheit wants to find a way to measure temperature accurately.
1800	The electric battery	Alessandro Volta wonders if chemical energy could be stored and used as electric energy.
1852	The first passenger elevator	Elisha Graves Otis wonders if he could develop a safe elevator with a brake to transport people up several floors.
1857	Pasteurizing process	Louis Pasteur wonders if heat could kill germs in milk to make it safer to drink.
1866	Dynamite	Alfred Nobel thinks there must be a way to make an explosive material that could be controlled.
1898	Discovery of radium	Marie and Pierre Curie wonder if radium could help cure diseases.
1985	Discovery of the sunken wreckage of the *Titanic*	Dr. Robert Ballard wants to locate the sunken ship at the bottom of the Atlantic Ocean.

GLOSSARY

bacteria Very, very tiny living things that can sometimes make you ill

bias When your own opinions affect your survey or experiment

chart A way of showing numbers in rows and columns. Also called a table

cluster balloon flight A flight using a large number of balloons

data Scientific information

filtration A process that helps remove solid bits from liquids

graph A diagram that can illustrate the results of an experiment. A graph has one measurement along the bottom, and another up the side

gravity The force that pulls things toward Earth

helium A gas that is lighter than air

hypothesis An educated guess about what an experiment will prove

journal A record of every step of an experiment

measurable Something that can be measured

Nobel Prize A special award given to people who do important things

observation Noticing something happening by using the five senses

oceanographer A scientist who studies oceans

polio A very infectious and serious disease

prediction When you say something is going to happen in the future

research Finding out facts about something

results The information that comes from an experiment

sample A group of people that listen to and discuss a scientist's question or idea

scientific method The way to do an experiment properly

specific Very detailed and exact

statement When you say something is definite

survey When you ask a lot of people what they know or think about something

technology Practical things created through science

ulcers A sore area on, or in the body

vaccine An injection that will protect you against a particular disease

FURTHER INFORMATION

Books
Why?, Catherine Ripley, Maple Tree Press, August 2004

The Everything Kids' Science Experiments Book, Tom Robinson, Adams Media, October 2001

Web sites
www.bbc.co.uk/schools/ks2bitesize/science/

www.macmillanmh.com/science/2011/student/na/grade3/index.html

INDEX